Date Due

DEC 3 0 1976			
JAN -6 1979	JUL -2 1993		
JAN 25 1979			
MAY 12 1979			
JUN -8 1979			
OCT -1 1979			
NOV 3 0 1979			
DEC 2 8 1979			
MAY -7 1981			
NOV 2 8 1981			
MAR 4 1982			
MAR 2 6 1982			
MAY 1 0 1983			
APR 1 8 1986			

12293

ANCIENT CEDAR BARK ROPE

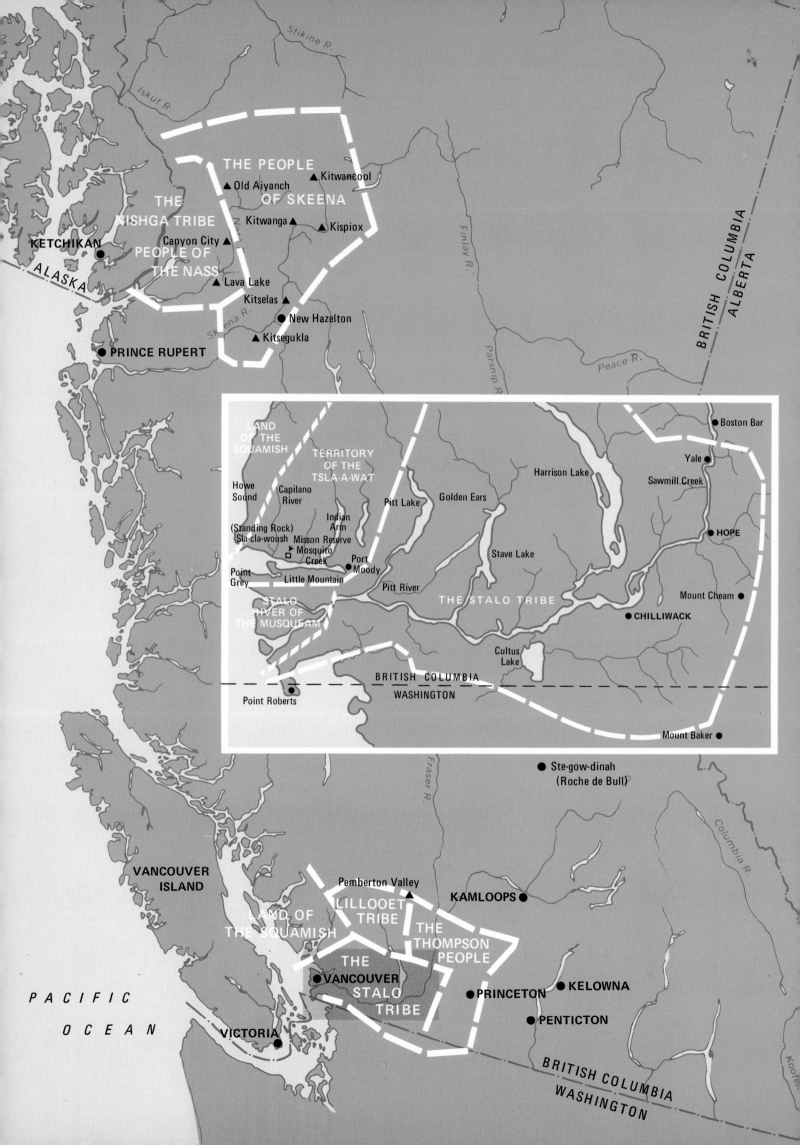

ABUNDANT

RIVERS

CHIEF DAN GEORGE EDITION

Photographs

Text & Design

By

ANTHONY CARTER

Hancock House, Saanichton, British Columbia, Canada

INDIAN HERITAGE SERIES
by ANTHONY CARTER

Volume 1   Somewhere Between 1966

Volume 2   This is Haida 1968. *Second Edition* 1971

Volume 3   Abundant Rivers 1972

Volume 4   From History's Locker 1973

Published by:
H A N C O C K   H O U S E,
3215 Island View Road,
Saanichton, British Columbia, Canada.

Historical photos courtesy of:
Provincial Museum and Archives, Victoria, B.C.
Vancouver City Archives, Vancouver, B.C.

Color separations: Quality Separations Ltd., Vancouver, B.C.
Typography: IBM "Selectric" Composer.
Printed by: Agency Press Ltd., Vancouver, B.C.
Bindery: Northwest Bindery Ltd., Vancouver, B.C.

INDEX

Salmon drying at Hell's Gate on the Fraser River.

Introduction

It was an unusually warm and sunny day in Klemtu, an Indian village and cannery town 300 miles up the coast from Vancouver. Twenty-eight bald eagles soared lazily over the harbour, waiting patiently for fish scraps and offal from the disgorging fish boats. My wife, Lyn, and I were torn between watching the eagles as they stooped for a drifting morsel and trying to find a way to move hundreds of pounds of our newly-arrived supplies from Klemtu to our summer destination fifty miles away. There were forty-five gallon barrels of gas for our floatplane and runabout, food and equipment to study eagles.

Hardly had we realized the extent of our plight than a softly-spoken fisherman leaned over the railing of his boat to say, "Brought your pet seal along too? You can't possibly get all that gear into a fourteen-foot boat and drive it as well as fly your plane. Can I take some of your supplies aboard the Wamega?"

Such was our introduction to Captain Anthony Carter. True, he loved the sea and was operating his own fishpacker, but it was obvious that he was a fisherman with a difference. Instead of the usual knife on the belt, Anthony carried a Hasselblad camera around his neck. Instead of being first in line to shoot, party and be merry when the fleet was in port, Anthony presented a warm reserved congeniality that deservedly earned him the position of "father confessor" to a hard-luck fisherman or distressed Indian maiden. The Indians said that "Wherever the Wamega sailed the waters calmed."

We saw Anthony many times that summer and have since shared an enriched friendship. It is with great honour that we are now able to present *Abundant Rivers,* · Volume Three of his Indian Heritage Series.

There is perhaps only one thing more fortuitous than a publisher having a good friend who is a highly skilled and respected photo-historian and that is knowing an extremely talented artist who can capture on canvas in an equally sensitive, meaningful and accurate way, the life of the Indian today. It is more than coincidental that the very moving paintings by Minn Sjolseth that we present here are a harmonious complement to Anthony Carter's photographs, for artist Minn Sjolseth is also Mrs. Minn Carter.

Much has been written about the "plight" of the Indian. More justly there should be many more volumes devoted to his contribution to our society, art and culture. And perhaps no man justifiably typifies the quiet dignity and success of his race more than Vancouver's own Chief Dan George. Anthony, Dan and Minn have been close friends these past years.

When Anthony said that Chief Dan had consented to write the foreword to *Abundant Rivers*, it seemed that the most appropriate tribute the Publishers could make to honour this man and his people was to present this special Chief Dan George edition.

Throughout the text we have attempted to give the phonetic spelling of the Indian names, followed in brackets by the more widely-used version.

David Hancock
Hancock House

Dedicated to my good friend
Chief Dan George

Foreword

Burrard Reserve, North Vancouver, B.C.
October 25, 1971

At last the culture of the Indians is revealed and exposed to the white man by this series of books written by a good friend of mine whom I have known for many years.

Many tribes' history is related in these books, the history of the tribes of the coast of B.C. If these books were in every school across Canada the white children would get the real history of the B.C. Indians.

The text books of the past have been so wrong. When the white man first came to this country he said that the Indians were heathens and savages which is so wrong, for thousands of years back our people knew of a Great Spirit and they had a prayer that was said every day by every Indian over the centuries.

The books written by my friend Anthony Carter should be read by every white man so they learn the true story of my people, and today as I sit here in my house and write these words that come right from my heart, sincerely and humbly, I hope this will reveal our true identity.

I have spoken

Chief Dan George

"You call me Chief . . ."

Of the many soliloquys which Chief Dan George has given, "You call me Chief. . ." is perhaps the most well known. This eloquent and moving speech was delivered in March of 1967 at the Playhouse Theatre, Vancouver, B.C.

You call me Chief and you do well for so I am. The blood of chieftains flows through my veins. I am a chief, but you ask where are my warriors with their feathered and painted faces. I am a chief, but my quiver has no arrows and my bow is slack. My warriors have been lost among the white man's cities. They have melted away into the crowds as once they did amid the forests. But this time they will not return. Yes, my quiver is empty, my bow is slack.

Ah, I could make new arrows and tighten my bow, but what little use it would be, for the arrow will not carry far as once it did, and the bow has been reduced to a plaything. What once a man's weapon is now a child's toy. I am a chief, but my power to make war is gone, and the only weapon left to me is my speech. It is only with tongue and speech that I can fight my people's war.

Today, my people are tempted to look to the past and say, "Behold our noble forebears." Perhaps it is pleasant to look to the ages gone by with brooding eyes and speak of the virility that once was ours. But the Redman can never again return to his campfires and forests. His campfires and forests no longer exist outside of his dreams. He will wear out many moccasins walking, searching, searching, and he will never return from the journey, for that which he seeks is no longer there.

It was during the first hundred years of Canada's nationhood that we met defeat. Broken by wars and disease we huddled on reserves and nursed our wounds. But our greatest wound was not of the flesh but in our spirit and in our souls. We were demoralized, confused, frightened. We were without weapons to defend ourselves, medicine to heal us, leaders to guide us. How easily despair comes when hope dies. How easily ambitions falter when goals slip from one's reach — like the end of a rainbow. How easily one says — "What's the use" — and dies inside himself. How easily drink, drugs and vice come when pride and personal worth are gone.

But after the winter's cold and the icy winds, life again flows up from the bosom of Mother Earth. And Mother Earth throws off dead stalks and withered limbs for they are useless. In their place new and strong saplings arise. Already signs of new life are arising among my people after our sad winter has passed. We have discarded our broken arrows and our empty quivers, for we know what served us in the past can never serve us again.

In unprecedented numbers our young men and women are entering the fields of education. There is longing in the heart of my people to reach out and grasp that which is needed for our survival. There is a longing among the young of my nation to secure for themselves and their people the skills that will provide them with a sense of purpose and worth. They will be our new warriors. Their training will be much longer and more demanding than it was in olden days. The long years of study will demand more determination, separation from home and family will demand endurance. But they will emerge with their hand held forward, not to receive welfare, but to grasp the place in society that is rightly ours.

The signs of this rebirth are all around us as more and more of our young men and women graduate from high school. And their numbers will grow and grow with the next hundred years until once again the Redman of Canada will stand firm and secure on his own two feet. With Pauline Johnson may I say
. . . .

> "Thus does the Redman stalk to death his foe,
> And sighting him, strings silently his bow,
> Takes his unerring aim, and straight and true,
> The arrow cuts in flight the forest through."

Painting of Chief Dan George by Minn Sjolseth
From her North West Coast Series.

Chief Dan George
"...a special kind of man"

Chief Dan George first stepped into the life of an actor when he played the part of "Ole Antoine" in the CBC Television production of the Caribou Series, a thirteen week adventure story of the life of an old Indian in British Columbia's Caribou Country. The series was a great success, and so was Dan. From then on he progressed steadily in his acting career.

His part as the star in the stage play, *The Ecstasy of Rita Joe*, a moving and singularly excellent story of the plight of an Indian girl in the big city, made him a legend in his own time. But Dan did not act in that play; to him it was too true to life to be acted as a stage play. George Ryga, the author of the drama, had given Dan a chance to express his feelings as an Indian, and when the curtain came down on the last act, Dan had made his point to perfection.

From *The Ecstasy of Rita Joe* Dan moved to greater things. A major part in the movie, *Smith* with actor Glen Ford was the break that he needed. From then on his success as film actor was assured. After co-starring with Dustin Hoffman in the movie, *Little Big Man*, Dan was chosen as a candidate for the highest award of the acting profession — the coveted Oscar — for his role as the best supporting actor of the year. He also received the New York Film Critics' Award, the award of the Canadian Council of Christians and Jews, and an honorary degree from the Simon Fraser University in Burnaby, B.C.

With all the honor and admiration that he has achieved, one might expect the man to have changed. But that is not possible. Chief Dan says very simply, "I do it all for the glory of the Indian people," and he means every word of it.

Dan was born on the Burrard Reserve along the north shore of Burrard Inlet in 1899. His father, Chief George Sla-Holt, was a true Tsla-a-wat Indian. This tribe inhabited the area of Burrard Inlet from a point at Lions Bay in West Vancouver across to Point Grey and all the shore lines east to Port Moody and Indian River. This tribe was distinctly different from the Squamish and Musqueam tribes to the north and south. In the legends of the Tsla-a-wat, it is said that many centuries ago, the tribe's ancestors came from far to the east over many mountains. This probably accounts for the difference in their language.

When he was very young, Dan was put into a boarding school. Here he realized that life among the Indian people was changing. He frequently thought of his father's wise words: "Education, my son, is the key to survival in this changing world."

At sixteen Dan left the boarding school and came home to the reserve to work with his father and older brother. They logged for a few years; the timber was good and it was a means to earn a living in those early years.

In 1919 Dan married Amy Jack, a Squamish girl. She was a truly wonderful mate for Dan and gave him love and encouragement for the fifty-two years of their married life. It was a great shock when she died in March of 1971. Amy George, a woman of great wit and charity, was a comfort to Dan and his constant companion. It is doubtful that he would have reached the levels of success that he has today if it had not been for her encouragement. She was dearly loved by all those who knew her.

Dan and Amy had six children, and at the time of writing there are 36 grandchildren — a happy progressive group of individuals with a very strong sense of family unity. Dan's youngest son, Lennie, is one member of the family that is likely to follow in his father's footsteps. He already has a number of successes in films and television plays; undoubtedly his fresh natural manner will ensure a successful acting career.

Dan has done many things in his 73 years. After the early days of logging, he worked as a longshoreman. In the late Forties, his family started their own musical band. This group of musicians, almost entirely self taught, was in great demand by local clubs. Together with Indian dancing groups, including their own tribal dancers, they contributed to the growing interest of the old native customs that have become part of our West Coast culture.

Through the experience of traveling with his band, Dan realized that a future lay in the field of entertainment. It was his stubborn perseverance that kept him going in the early lean years of his acting career. But as someone said during the filming of the Caribou Series, "Dan is a special man; he is a great human being." Chief Dan has unmistakable humanitarian qualities that are rare in our times. Everyone with whom he speaks is a little richer when Dan leaves, and he is never too busy to stop to say a few words.

Route of Adventure

Who is changed or changing
in this world?
All beauty still remains throughout
the land for all time hence,
and we, the feeble, grasping ants
that crawl along the valley floor
will change and make our ways
as nature smiles or frowns her
weathered face at us,
the fools.

Guardian of the harbor, a symbol of honor for the tribes of old. A majestic and unique landmark for the people of the great city of Vancouver today.

Sla-cla-woush (Standing rock)

The name Sla-cla-woush means Standing Rock, and the legend of this landmark goes back in the history of our Indian people far beyond the memory of the oldest of those who are still in our midst today.

It is interesting that the different tribes of this area have similar stories of its origin. The Squo-umish (Squamish) from far up Howe Sound tell of the Cha-um-sik, three men who were roaming the world to make changes for the betterment of the people. One day they came upon a man bathing in the inlet at this point. Approaching him they said, "Young man, you must go out of the water and let us pass." "No," replied the young man, "I must finish my bathing," and with that he went on scrubbing himself with a sponge of cedar fibre.

Three times the Cha-um-sik asked him to retreat to the shore, but he refused. One of the men in the canoe turned to the other two and said, "The young man is very brave, and if it is so important for him to keep his body clean that he would stand against we three, I think he should set an example for all time to come; that to be clean of body and mind is all important."

With united agreement they changed the young man into a rock, standing erect as he did before them, with a little growth on the top for his hair. Sla-cla-woush, or Standing Rock, is a fitting name for this unique landmark, standing at the harbour entrance watching the volumes of history slowly fill the shelves of the past.

LAND OF THE SQUAMISH

The Squamish tribe at one time occupied only Howe Sound and the Squamish Valley. The tribe has now spread out over a much larger area to include the reserves of Capilano and the North Vancouver mission site at Mosquito Creek.

These people were excellent canoe builders and highly skilled in the art of weaving baskets and garments.

Although no totem carving existed in the tribe's pre-white history, they have borrowed the designs of their northern neighbors and today carry out a limited amount of carving.

Mountain Solitude

BLACK TUSK

Part of Garibaldi Provincial Park and land of the Squamish. From glacial ice the waters flow to make our rivers in abundance. This was the land of the Squamish hunter where he pursued the wily mountain goat for wool to make his Squoquith (cape) or blankets.

Outlet at Garibaldi Lake

Mari Jack, wife of August Jack, was born in Nanaimo of that tribe in 1880.

August Jack, or Kahts-Lanock, was born of Squamish parents living temporarily in Stanley Park. He was 99 years and 7 months old when he passed away in 1967. Kahts-Lanock was also the last of the medicine men.

The very beautiful dogwood, an unforgettable sight along the wooded shores of the B.C. coast.

Legend of the Mink

It is hard sometimes to describe a legend, and this one is no exception. Here it is, essentially the same as it was told to me one very pleasant afternoon at the house of one of our most interesting and charming oldtimers, Dominic Charlie, a full-blooded Squamish Indian, with a wit and humor to match his very agile 84 years.

The story begins with a mink (Khi-ach) and a flounder who is his cousin. They were in a canoe one day, paddling along the shore, when a whale came up to them and nosed the canoe. "Go away," said the mink, "you are nothing more than a place for barnacles to grow on." Whereupon the whale swallowed the canoe with its two occupants.

After a most uncomfortable trip down into the whale's stomach, the mink and flounder searched around for a means of escape, and as the mink moved about he kept bumping into something. Finally, in desperation, he cut the object down as it was dangling from the top of the cavern.

This was a stroke of luck for he severed the heart of the great whale.

Immediately, the great whale began flopping this way and that and swimming in all directions.

"Since you are going to die," the mink called to the whale, "you may as well swim up to the beach so that we can get out." Whereupon the whale marooned himself on the shore.

As it turned out, the place where they landed was near a village of people who wished to kill the mink. Knowing he was in the whale, they climbed up on to its head and enlarged the air hole in the whale so that they could catch the mink when he tried to escape.

The mink and flounder heard the commotion going on outside and feared for their lives.

Turning to the flounder the mink said, "Hang on to me very tightly and I will jump clear of the people into the deep water and we will escape." And so they went out and the people were not quick enough to catch them.

Many days later the mink was swimming alone by the shore of an island when he looked up and saw a small cloud close to the water. It was the most beautiful cloud he had ever seen. It was like a beautiful wistful maiden and he fell in love at the sight of such a lovely thing.

"Come to me," he called, "and I will marry you." And the cloud called back: "I cannot marry you, for I must go as the wild wind calls and you could not stay with me."

"Please, my love," he cried, "I will hold on tightly and follow you all over the earth." And so he did, but soon a storm came up and the lovely cloud tumbled and turned and raced across the sky until the mink could no longer hold on. In a short time he fell to the ground and was killed.

This seemed to be the end of Khi-ach the mink, but in those days the raven Skaw-ouck had great powers and, looking down to the earth, he saw his old friend, Khi-ach, lying dead on the ground.

Slowly, he circled down, calling his chant: "Skaw-ouck, Skaw-ouck," as he came to rest beside his friend. Very quickly he made a medicine and poured it over the now decaying body of Khi-ach. In a moment life stirred in the mink, and soon he was up — as well as ever. "Many thanks to you my friend, Skaw-ouck," he said, as his feathered friend flew off into the forest.

In the weeks that followed the mink became lonely and one day, as he drifted in and out of the rocks along the shore, he saw some extremely pretty heads of kelp. It was like a beautiful maiden's head with flowing hair streaming out in the currents of the sea.

"Marry me," he called, "oh lovely maiden of the sea. Your beauty must be mine, please marry me."

And the kelp maiden answered: "How I wish that I could, but I am torn by the tides. All day the currents swirl about me and you would not be able to stay with me."

"But I will hold on very tight," he said. And so they were married.

But alas, her words were true, and soon he had to depart for she tossed and swirled in the sea and he could not stay.

Sadly, Khi-ach roams the beaches today, and as you see him among the rocks and watch his silken brown body slip from one crevice to another, he is searching, searching for a love that will stay.

SQUAMISH RIVER

For centuries the Squamish tribes hunted and fished for food along these shores. Hunger was uncommon in this valley of the bountiful river.

Dominic Charlie, named after his grandfather Yulc-Whaltin, the famous Weather Prophet.

Yulc-Whaltin

Dominic Charlie's grand-dad was a man of extraordinary perception, and his ability to foretell the future was well known among the Indian people of the lower coast.

The story of this gift is an interesting one.

Yulc-Whaltin was a man of the wilderness, and most of his life was spent among the mountainous ranges and game-filled valleys of the Squamish territory. One evening, as he sat by a campfire many miles from his lodge, a sound of rushing wind and thunder filled the air about him. Quietly he sat and waited, for his sixth sense told him someone was coming.

Very soon there was a sound behind him as though a person was moving toward him; and this was true, because a stick poked him in the back and a voice said: "Why do you stay away from your people for such a long time?" Yulc-Whaltin replied: "I have a wife and family to feed and not all my people are hunters, so I must provide meat for many mouths in my village."

The voice spoke again and said: "Here is a scroll for your guidance. In it are things to help you. Those things that are to come you will now know, and will be able to direct your people in ways that are good. Keep it for all your life and heed what it says." And with that, the strange night caller was gone.

It is said this scroll is buried with Yulc-Whaltin. Many people have tried to find it, but its whereabouts remain a secret; perhaps it is better this way.

Black Bear (The Man from Squamish)

Squai-Squai is the name of a mask, found among the Tsla-a-wat, Musqueam and Squamish tribes. Originally a Tsla-a-wat symbol of power and authority, it came by marriage into the families of Musqueam and Squamish tribesmen. To this day it is used on ceremonial occasions by the ancestors of the man who married the daughter of Si-tai-a-much, or Squai-Squai as he was later called when the mask was found by him in a fallen cedar tree.

It all started many years ago in the Squamish valley when a young man set out to look for a wife away from his own band. Unfortunately his name is not remembered by any of the people living today, so we will call him Black Bear for this was the crest of his tribe.

Far up the Squamish River among the jagged cliffs along the shore lived the band of Black Bear, and for some years now the village had no young women eligible for marriage. Black Bear was now a grown man and he knew if he was to have a wife of his age he must go away from his village. Back in his boyhood days he had heard of a tribe to the east, somewhere, it was said, over three valleys away.

To the young man, in those far-off days, it was like travelling to the moon, but he was young and strong and he thought even if it takes two or three summers he must go.

And so he went, bidding his family farewell, not knowing if he would ever see them again.

As the days passed and Black Bear slowly travelled eastward he was happy, for in some way he knew his mission would not be in vain. Weeks turned into months. Along the way he killed mountain goats and stayed for many days in one place to dry the meat so that he could carry it more easily.

Sometimes he found it necessary to make detours around impossible gorges and mountain peaks, and this made the journey very long, but Black Bear was tough and made light of his hardships.

Finally, after a trek of almost two years, he found himself on the shores of the Tsla-a-wat (Indian Arm) opposite the village of Belcarra. This was a very powerful tribe, rich in terms of natural abundance and under the wise and kind guidance of Waut-Sauk, the chief.

As Black Bear stood on the shores of this strange and beautiful inlet he knew he was once again at the sea and he was elated at his success. His dreams were beginning to come true at last.

Seeing some activity out on the water he called, and soon a canoe with four young boys came up to him. With a little difficulty he made it understood to them what his mission was.

But they said, "There are no young women at our village who you may take as a wife. You are too late, all of them are already given in marriage. But at the home of Squai-Squai at the big narrows, a very beautiful young woman waits in her father's house for a suitable husband. If you will stay here, we will go to him tomorrow and tell him of your story."

Happily Black Bear agreed, and as the young boys sped away in their canoe he settled down on the mossy bank to rest and await their return.

Very early the following morning he saw a canoe moving swiftly on the outgoing tide. In a very short time it disappeared around the old village site to the south of him (Roche Point) and he knew his message would soon be told to Squai-Squai.

Sometime in the afternoon the canoe came back around the point and went on to the village. Black Bear was puzzled. What could be wrong? Had he been refused? He had not long to wait for an answer for even as he pondered these things the canoe appeared again, coming toward him with another canoe in tow.

As they pulled the second canoe alongside and glided up to the beach, one of them said, "The young woman awaits you. We will take your pack of goat meat and yourself to the man Squai-Squai so that you may claim his daughter as your wife."

"We told him your story and he is honoured that a young man of such courage and endurance should take his daughter in marriage. As we talk here a feast is being prepared in expectation of your arrival."

Black Bear was delighted and he thanked them a thousand times for being so kind to him.

Quickly split planks were tied across the two canoes to form a platform for his bundles of dried goat meat. And as they moved out from the beach he took his place at the front of the bundles as guest of honour for the trip to meet his bride-to-be.

At the house of Squai-Squai preparations were being completed for the arrival of the new son-in-law. Being a rich family, nothing was spared to make the best possible impression on the young man. After all was complete, a final touch of grandeur was given by unrolling the tremendous goat hair carpet that reached from the house to the beach for the young man to walk upon, and at the end of the carpet that remained in the house, the daughter sat in her finest attire waiting for the young man to come.

Before the sun had set Black Bear arrived and claimed his bride. Everyone was happy and these people took to him as their own. It was a time of great rejoicing for one and all. As the days passed, Black Bear thanked the great spirit, Hai-is, for giving him the strength and courage to fulfill his mission.

Although Black Bear was contented in his new surroundings, he became lonesome for his own people and eventually the father-in-law said: "My son, I can see you are longing to see your own people, so go to them now. We will miss you and our daughter, but our wish is that you should be happy."

So Black Bear and his wife embarked upon the long canoe trip to the Squamish River and in time arrived at the camp of his own tribe. They set up their own house and remained in the village, but not for long, for shortly after their return Black Bear became ill and died. They had no children and eventually the young widow returned to her own people.

A year or two after her return home a Musqueam man became very fond of her and in time they went away together as man and wife. Little is known of them from then on, and somewhere back in time this wisp of history faded into oblivion.

SQUAMISH RIVER

Along the high ridges above the river the mountain sheep and goat were hunted for their beautiful white coats and fat nourishing meat. Only the most skilful hunters pursued these swift and wary animals.

Spirit of Wountie

The Squamish River holds many secrets to the history and legend of its peaceful valley, and it is likely that we will never know more than a very few of the stories that could be told. However, among the ones we do know, this story of the greedy fisherman is interesting and most certainly holds a moral that is as valid today as it was when told in the lodges of the Indian villages centuries ago.

As the legend goes, there is a curious rock in the river that stands guard to see that no-one takes more fish than is needed, and to make sure that an equal share is had by all the people in the valley.

One day a man came down to fish for food in the river and as he approached he saw that the fish were swimming upstream in great numbers. "Good fortune is mine," he thought, "I will soon have enough fish to take to my family," and he hurriedly set his net across the stream. In no time at all he had all he required, but the sight of so many fat, gleaming fish around him made him greedy and he set the net again. Waiting on the shore for a few moments he

returned to lift his net, but to his great surprise it was full of sticks and pieces of wood. Thinking he must have set his net poorly he made his net fast in another place. But again when he lifted it, it was full of sticks and driftwood.

"What have I done wrong," he said aloud to himself. "There are still great numbers of fish swimming up the stream. I cannot understand what is the matter."

Taking his net to shore he sat down to think. Looking up the river he could see the fish still jumping and finning their way upstream. Then he saw the rock, the tall quiet sentinel of the river's bounty. The spirit of Wountie was in this rock to watch over the fish. Now the fisherman knew what was wrong. He had forgotten for a moment and tried to take more than his share but the spirit of Wountie had turned the fish in his net to sticks. Quickly he got to his feet and gathered the fish he had caught, vowing he would never again be greedy and take more than he had need of.

KO-CU-TUM (BUMPING NOISE)

Most certainly one of the more beautiful displays of nature along the shores of Howe Sound is Ko-cu-tum, meaning Bumping Noise, and now called Shannon Falls.

The Squamish tribe in the valley named it for the vibrant bumping noise it made as thousands of gallons of water tumbled over the rocks to the stream below. Over the years, men of all nations have paused to look in wonder at this gem of nature, a poem in a veil of silver spray.

THE
LILLOOET
TRIBE

It is in the beautiful Pemberton Valley with its towering snow-capped peaks, broad green meadows and sparkling rivers that the Lillooet Indians live. This peaceful area has always provided the Lillooets with an affulent way of life. They did no trading with their neighbours and were a very self-sufficient people. Nature supplied their every need — fish, wildlife, and forests were in abundance.

The present tribe lives on the Mount Currie Reserve. This reservation is one of the largest in Canada with a population of 900. The Indian village is a beautiful sight with old hand-hewn loghouses lining the main street, resembling a century-old page from the history books.

It is difficult to understand how an entire village can retain its character of the past in our modern complex world. It is hoped that the changes that surely must come will not spoil the charm and antiquity of the area.

Pemberton Valley, a rich and fertile area ringed by snow-capped peaks. This is the home of a band of Lillooet Indian people. (Mount Currie Reserve)

Sheila Wallace, a pretty example of the new generation.

Theresa Gabriel 86 years old. An old timer in the valley, she has watched history unfold around her.

Old buildings of another age make sharp contrast to the children's plastic toys.

Cornelius Sam, a cheerful humorous fellow.

Matilda Jim, 106 years old. One of the village's most active basket makers. She spends her days weaving to meet a constant demand for her wares.

TERRITORY OF THE TSLA-A-WAT

The Tsla-a-wat tribe, now living on the north shore of Burrard Inlet was once large and powerful. Their old tribal territory extended from Lions Bay across to Point Grey and included all the waters of English Bay and Burrard Inlet east to Port Moody and Indian River. Many small bands of the tribe lived in this area, and at one time their numbers probably exceeded two or three thousand.

Their language or dialect was distinctly different from their neighbors, the Squamish and Musqueam. However, in recent years intermarriage among these three tribes has eliminated all but the Squamish tongue.

The Tsla-a-wat band, now numbering only about a hundred and twenty, live east of the Second Narrows on land they have owned for centuries; and the present chief, John Lewis George is the kind of man who will ensure the preservation of the tribal lands

Where H.M.S. Discovery is today was once an old burial site of native people from the villages of Stanley Park.

Si-tai-a-much (Squai-squai)

The name of Si-tai-a-much belonged to the head man of the band of Tsla-a-wat, who lived at what is now known as Lumberman's Arch. He was a man of considerable wealth, being a highly skilled canoe builder.

His canoe building was done mostly on the shores of Ach-a-tchu (Beaver Lake). Here the magnificent red cedars were an inspiration and source of raw material for the artist.

One day as he laboriously felled a huge cedar for a new canoe, he was dismayed that it split from butt to tip as it hit the ground. Looking carefully along the split for some way to redeem this great tree, he found inside a curious mask and several strange seashells.

Carefully, he removed the mask from the tree, and as he held it he felt a new power rising in himself, which made him very happy indeed, for now his family would be safe from all perils. To honour this great event he changed his name to Squai-Squai, for such was the name of the mask.

Squai-Squai eventually came to be very widely known for his extraordinary powers as a medicine man, and this strange power was passed on to his daughter when the mask was willed to her upon his death.

As the pages of time have turned, the mask has seen many changes in the destiny of the Indian people.

MOSQUITO CREEK, NORTH VANCOUVER

Once a well-known clam bed and fishing area for the Tsla-a-wat people, this area is now a commercial marina owned and operated by the resident North Vancouver Indians.

CAPILANO RIVER

It's doubtful if a day goes by without a salmon being caught in this interesting and historical river. It was here in the crystal waters of this beautiful stream that the spawning salmon were taken by the hundreds for winter food. The meat was dried and cured in the sun and the roe stored in boxes of cedarwood to age.

Once a major coho spawning ground, modern commercial fishermen have now reduced the run to negligible proportions.

However, it is still an enticing river for the sportsman, producing its share of food for those who care to cast a line across its sparkling, coaxing ripples.

MISSION CHURCH

The Mission Church in North Vancouver is one of the oldest churches on the Lower Mainland and its twin spires form a notable landmark for the area.

The Mission Reserve where the church stands is probably one of the oldest sites of Christian teaching among the Indians of the lower coast of British Columbia.

It was here in the very early days of the white settlers of Vancouver that the Roman Catholic priests held services on the beach. As the Squamish people came down from Howe Sound and the Squamish River valley to take part in the industry of the new cities of Vancouver and Moodyville, it seemed quite logical that they should build homes at this site to be near the teachers of this newfound religion, and to

share in the excitement of the white man's activity. Although by old tribal law the land belonged to the Tsla-a-wat nation it was a time of change and the old terms of reference no longer seemed valid. If you were living on a piece of land when the land was surveyed, there was a good chance that you would own it by sheer weight of occupation.

The Capilano Reserve people are merely an expansion of the original groups of Squamish people who migrated down to the Mission Reserve after the establishment of the Church.

Viewing this panorama of Vancouver it is hard to realize that less than a century ago it was virgin forest. This was the land of Waut-Sauk the great Tsla-a-wat chief.

The Canada geese were part of a lovely natural world before our time.

The yellow Arum Lily or Skunk Cabbage, a colorful harbinger of spring. The Indians used to wave the large leaves of this plant over the fire to make them limp, then wrap food in them for storage.

Wild Rose, a cheerful sight against the mass of green forest. It was also a valuable food source for native people.

*Beginning of old tribal boundaries — Howe Sound,
home of the great Squamish tribe.*

LITTLE MOUNTAIN

This ridge was a part of the old tribal boundaries between the Tsla-a-wat and Musqueam tribes.

ENGLISH BAY

It was here that Waut-Sauk, great Chief of the Tsla-a-wat nation, came out to meet Captain Vancouver in the year 1792.

STALO (FRASER)
river of the Musqueam People

The Musqueam were a very large tribe. They lived along the shores of the mighty Fraser from where the river divides into the north and south arms, westward to the Gulf of Georgia.

This was truly a land of plenty for here the great runs of salmon entered the river for the long migration to the spawning grounds. In the confines of the river, they were easy to catch; in addition there were clams and crabs to be had for the taking. Halibut and oolichan were also caught in their season.

The abundant food supply and a temperate climate made the Musqueam a peaceful and friendly people. It was at the present Musqueam reserve site that the explorer Simon Fraser went ashore to erect a cairn marking the end of his journey down the river that now bears his name.

Watch the river flow my love
    each ripple speaks a message as it
    passes on the way.
It tells of days of bygone youth
    when mother took our hand,
    and walked with us along
    the banks,
    to write our names with
    sticks of wood
    in moist and crumbly sand.
Remember where the little pool
    lay quiet, in the shade?
    And summer days so hot
    and still, would send us
    running there to wade.
The stones were grumbly underfoot
    our feet so pale, a funny look
    as velvet water passed them by.
    How wonderful, you said, and we
    never knew how sweet and rich
    these days could be
    'til now.

Stone weights, personal ornaments and some of the
jade cutting tools used by the Indian people all along
the British Columbia coast.
(Philip Carter Collection)

An exceptional collection of arrow and spear heads.
(Stephen Carter Collection.)

The Musqueam children have bathed and swam in this part of the Fraser River since time began. Will it always be that way?

The canoes of these two ancient races rest on the sandy shore of an historic river, the mighty Stalo, as children of the new world share a common happiness, unaware that history lies just beneath the sand at their feet.

POINT GREY

From this ancient landmark many eyes have beheld this beautiful vista. Ancient man as he stood here could in no way have envisioned what was to come to this land of snow-capped peaks and sparkling water; but we, the people of today, can look back and know what it was like in the centuries past.

Nature is unchanging and mankind cannot improve upon it. His greatest endeavor can only make the very local scene a little different. When the first adventurers sailed into this harbor and planted the seeds of a white civilization, that is all that really happened. The grandeur of the mountain ranges and sparkling waters changing from blue-green to tints of brown as the tides ebb and flow about the river's mouth; these things remain the same.

Our thanks for this, the heritage of nature.

THE
STALO
TRIBE

Here, at the junction of the Fraser and Pitt Rivers, the tribes of Stalo and Musqueam met, and intermarriage of the two nations was not uncommon, so that the people today in this upper valley area are often a mixture of the two.

Tribes to the south and north of the Stalo also came into the area, trading goods and visiting during the days of summer rest and ceremonies.

Although the white man has brought about many changes in the ways of life for the Indian people, the scene is almost the same as it was centuries ago: the proud mountain peaks still look down on a restless river, and the basket weavers still roam the cedar bluffs along the valley searching for roots to split and weave, to leave behind someday a pretty thing, or a word in the page of history.

The mysterious Pitt River flows out of the dark valley of the Golden Ears mountain range. Somewhere back in these mountains the Shumask gold lies hidden; perhaps its whereabouts will remain a mystery for all time.

*Mrs. Charles remembers well the early white settlers
coming to claim the land of her forefathers.*

Unwinding itself through the narrow gorges of the canyon, the Stalo enters the broad seaward valley in an uncertain sweeping silver ribbon, to find its way quietly to the sea.

House of Shadows

Long ago in the mythology of the Halkomelem tribes of the Fraser River, the story tellers would sit at the evening campfire and tell the lovely old legends of their ancestors. Among the tales for the little children, this one about the House of Shadows must surely have delighted both young and old.

It seems that all the people of the valley had a shadow of one kind or another: the shadows were really other people who just attached themselves to you. Now this arrangement was rather pleasant, because you always had company on a hike or some other mission. To be sure, the cloudy days were a bit awkward because shadows don't show too well, but the real problem was at night, for as soon as the sun went down the shadow became separated from its companion, and sorting out your right shadow the next morning was really quite a task.

Then, one day the chief said to his shadow: "My friend, please do my people and me a favor. As you know, we have trouble to find you each day when the sun comes up, and it would be so much easier if you would only get together in one place overnight. Only this morning my little son spent a long time searching for his shadow because he could not remember where he had left it the night before."

"Very well," the shadow said, "we will gather each night at the old deserted house at the river's edge, and this way we can have a nice visit among ourselves and you and your people will know where to find us in the morning."

So, from that day on, the shadows gathered to visit in the old house, and if you should go there now at night you will find a few of the old shadows still lurking among its beams, waiting to be claimed by someone — because shadows live forever, like stories, if they are nice!

Fraser River as it leaves the canyon at Hope.

Silver Creek, a fisherman's delight.

PETER'S FARM

Granny Peters is a happy, industrious soul if I ever saw one. Her joy of life shows in her work. Here, split cedar roots, as fine as cotton, are carefully woven into a basket. Her work is that of an artist.

The basket I saw that sunny afternoon was about twenty inches across and a little deeper from top to bottom. It was one of the best examples of the art of basketry I have ever seen.

"I like to see it grow," she said. "It took four months to make the big one, and I walked all over the valley collecting the roots and material for the dyes.

"When you are young it is easy, but at 77 the hills are a little higher and the miles a little longer. Must be getting old, I guess."

And as the afternoon went along, she told of all the little things that go into making a basket. Once the roots are gathered they have to be split into hundreds of tiny strands of cedar fibre, some a little wider, some a little thicker — all are needed to make a pattern. They must be dyed too with the juice of red willow root and alder — red, brown, white and black. This lovely old lady works to make something pretty, and she succeeds so well.

Yes, I will remember Granny Peters and her baskets for a long, long time.

Granny Peters — Basket Weaver First Class.

MOUNT CHEAM

Great Lady is the Indian name bestowed upon this magnificent peak of the Coast Range. The Indian people of the Valley of Stalo have always highly regarded this beautiful mountain. From its snowy slopes, mountain goat supplied them with long silky wool for blankets and garments. Deer abounded along the lower wooded hills to provide food for the many people who lived along the river banks.

Looking up from the broad green valley floor on a clear spring day, the bright green specks of budding birch give way to the darker green of fir and hemlock; purple velvet shadows of the uppermost cliffs blend into the crisp white crown of the peak: truly a diamond tiara for the Great Lady.

Mount Baker, a snow-capped sentinel for the beautiful Fraser Valley.

Reflections

The Fraser River at Hope

Sawmill Creek, one of the thousands of mountain streams that build a river.

*"Hundreds of remains" How very true – and the spirit
of these people of long ago still fills the canyon of the
mighty Stalo with their mystery. Surely the way of
the early white travellers down to the sea would have
been more difficult without their help.*

A century-old church at Yale, the touch of a strange religion for the tribes along the Stalo.

ABUNDANT RIVER

The mighty Fraser tumbles its way to the sea. From quiet eddy to roaring rapid the power of nature stills the voice of man as the canyon walls resound in sympathy.

Kristina Bob, 78 years, Boston Bar: Patient hands that toil till work is done. For many years the calloused palms have thrust the awl to make another stitch of root, and slowly, round and round it grows, till the shape is formed like something living from her touch. A little love and tender care — the work of patient hands.

Mely Peters, one of the best blanket weavers in the Fraser Valley.

Looking north, the winding path of the mighty Fraser rises out of the narrow canyon.

THE
THOMPSON
PEOPLE

The Indian people along the Thompson are the last of the true river dwellers before entering the interior. They are in a way a mixture of two cultures, having adapted many of the coastal arts and crafts to their own particular needs. Also, they share a language similarity with many of the interior tribes. Their history is a very old one and recent excavations within this territory have proven that these people were a culturally advanced race many thousands of years ago.

The sparkling waters of the Thompson River show a marked contrast to the turbulent and muddy Fraser.

The dragon-fly, used by the Indian people in story and art.

The Yellow Bell, one of the many edible plants of the Thompson River area. These beautiful little flowers grow in abundance all over the dry areas of our province but suffer from thoughtless over picking by the traveling public.

Mountain Sheep. These animals provided a good part of the diet of the Thompson people long ago.

Happiness is a child's heritage, especially a little girl's.

The charm and dignity of an ageless culture reflect in the face of this young Indian girl.

Helmcken River winds its way through a million-year old gorge to find its destiny in the mighty Stalo.

Helmcken Falls, a wilderness wonder in Wells Gray Park.

Ste-gow-dinah (Roche de Bull). Magnificent mountain
at the headwaters of the Skeena River.

THE PEOPLE OF SKEENA
(Gitskan and Tsimshian)

Gits-ka-Shaan (Ksan) or Skeena River means the River that Flows from the Misty Clouds. Gits-ka-Shaan is the name of the tribe at Kitsegukla, now commonly referred to as Gitskan. It is also the name generally used for the dialect of all the people of the Skeena above Kitselas Canyon.

Ste-gow-dinah, or Big Mountain, as the Gitskan people called it, is named Roche de Bull on the white man's maps, but whatever it is called, the mountain is always there, looking down on a beautiful and provident valley. Here is the junction of many rivers, the Bulkley, Skeena, Kispiox and many other smaller streams, all giving their share of abundance to the people who live along the shores.

The Indian people of Kitwancool, Kispiox, Kitwanga, Kitsegukla, Kitselas and others have taken the silver bounty of these rivers for centuries. The great runs of salmon that migrate yearly through these crystal waters have always been the main food source of the Gitskan tribes in the valley, and today it is essentially no different.

In the fall, when the runs of salmon reach their peak, the Indian people can still be found netting and gaffing fish to be smoked and dried. It takes a lot of fish to feed a family over a long winter, and although there is a lot of good-natured fun taking place among the groups as the harvest goes on, it is still a very serious affair. Meat from moose, deer, bear, goat and smaller game is added to the diet later in the year, but fish is always the most dependable of all food sources.

This area of many rivers (now widely known as the Hazeltons), is the end of river navigation. From here to the interior the trade between the tribes was seriously hampered by lack of water transport. Every article of trade goods had to be back-packed. Ooli-chan grease was carried in wooden boxes weighing as much as a hundred pounds or more, and it was the great amounts of this oil being carried over the inland route that accounts for the name Grease Trail being used to identify the pack route to the coastal rivers.

The Tsimshian tribes of the coast proper extended up the Skeena to villages below Kitselas Canyon, the Kitselas village people being the first of the interior Gitskans up river from the sea.

Of all the coastal tribes, the Tsimshian group was the most outstanding as traders or middle men. In the exchange of goods from one tribe to another, they traded with the Haida of the Queen Charlotte Islands: oolichan grease and furs for the great Haida canoes and other small commodities, and these in turn were traded to the Gitskans for goods from the interior. It is notable that in those days the women of the tribes conducted most of the business transactions.

The totem carving of the Gitskan differs considerably from the coast tribes such as Haida, Kwakiutl and Nootka. Generally, the Gitskan used much smaller trees, and in particular the carvings differed radically in design.

Many of the totems were carved along the complete length of the pole, and yet some had no carving at all with perhaps only a bird or other symbol secured at the top.

The clan crests are readily identifiable. Most of the other symbolic figures are either unknown or without meaning to the Indian people today. This gap in the culture of these tribes can be attributed almost entirely to the lack of understanding by the white people in the early years of our history on this coast. It is only during the last decade that the cultural and historic art of the Indian peoples of this continent has been understood and given the high status it richly deserves.

The northern Timber Wolf, nature's most efficient,
yet maligned, hunter.

A considerable number of the Gitskan people belonged to the Wolf clan. Here Gladys Gunanoot displays her tribal emblem, the Wolf, on a very fine example of a button blanket robe.

Blackfish pole at Hagwilget near Hazelton.

View of the Skeena valley from old Hazelton. The village of New Hazelton is seen at the base of the mountains.

David Gunanoot, Chief of Gitsga-gas (Gitskan). His Indian name is Ne-gap (ten frogs on a log). Chief Gunanoot is the son of the famous figure of history, Simon Gunanoot, who was hunted by the police for twenty years for a murder he did not commit. The plight of Simon Gunanoot as a fugitive for those long and terrible years is an outstanding example of the lack of understanding between the authorities and the Indian people.

Kathleen Gunanoot, sister to David. A proud and resolute woman. Her Indian name is We-na-gits, meaning Big Wolverine.

Interior of the new Ksan Village long house at Hazelton, B.C. It is an outstanding example of the old culture of the west coast Indian people.

Old poles at Kispiox Village. The village is located at the junction of the Kispiox and Skeena Rivers, one of the world's best salmon fishing areas.

The Skeena River from Kispiox village site.

KISPIOX

The original name was Kis-pa-iox which means Hiding Place.

Elvis Harry Wilson, a truly delightful little boy from Kispiox.

Fallen pole at Kispiox.

Bear pole at Kitwancool.

"WINTER SOLITUDE"

Probably the oldest existing totem in the world today. At the village of Kitwancool.
Painting by Minn Sjolseth. From her North West Coast Series.

The old grave house has fallen to decay leaving some of this long departed soul's worldly goods exposed once more to the light of day.

It was customary among most of the Indian tribes to bury the prized possessions of an individual along with his remains. This ancient rite is no longer practised.

Chief Ernie Hyjmar's pole, the only carved pole remaining by the river at the old village site of Kitsegukla.

This very old pole carved with a human figure and birds
is a striking land mark in the village of Kitsegukla.

A beautifully carved memorial pole. Its design and
character are outstanding. It is the first pole located
at the north end of the village of Kitsegukla.

A fine example of a frog pole — one of the many clan crests at Kitsegukla.

This well-carved pole belongs to Mr. Russell, one of the councilors at Kitsegukla. The predominant long-billed bird is a mythical figure called "Weneel".

Kitselas Canyon with Ring Bolt Island in centre. It was here that the early sternwheelers often met their doom on the rapids of this canyon.

Last fragment of house post from the village of Chief Kitselas.

THE NISHGA TRIBE
people of the Naas

The Nass River to the north of the Skeena is another historic, and fortunately still remote river. The Indian name for it is Nishga and along its shores are still a few of the old villages. The most notable of these is Old Aiyanch, or Gitlakdamiks as it was originally named.

Nearby Canyon City, an incongruous name for an isolated Indian village, was originally called Gitwanuscolth by the tribes along the Nass. It can only be approached from land by a swinging foot bridge which crosses the river at this narrow point.

The Nass river valley is one of the most beautiful of all the northern areas. Towering mountain peaks, sparkling lakes and streams afford abundant land in which to hunt and fish. The Nishga people live in a natural paradise and they know it. Since time began it has been their land, it must always be that way.

Lava Lake, headwaters lake of a Nass tributary.

Hundreds of acres of lava beds on the banks of the Naas River.

NASS RIVER — end of the lava beds.

Oolichans drying in the sun near the Nass River.

OLD AIYANCH

Abel Derek at Gitlakdamix, now called Old Aiyanch
"I am just a common man."

The last remaining pole at Old Aiyanch.

Bessie Haizinqua — a proud young Nishga woman. Walking along the pathway through the old village of Aiyanch. She carried a bowl of bear meat; the scene was primitive and beautiful.

OLD AIYANCH

The splendid old buildings are falling into decay. The inhabitants were moved unwillingly to the south of the river — far from their beloved Nass.

A drop of rain, a millionfold
to gather strength along the way
The little creek becomes a stream
to multiply another day
And soon, a river's might is born
as water from the land is torn
to fall in cascades to the sea,
Abundant Rivers must always be.

ANCIENT CEDAR BARK ROPE